Dreams can either make you, or break you. It all depends on what you see, how you interpret your dreams, and add them; your dreams to your life and the life of others. Dreams are education tools, ways for you to glance; see into the past, present, and future; what's to come.

Many people do not believe in dreams, but that's okay. It's not all who have sight to see; the gift of life to tell.

Therefore, battles rage due to the lies of men; humans.
People live in lies; confusion.
The death toll rise.
Casualties many.

Confusion set in.
Many are dazed.
Many could not decipher.

Carnage is coming this I know. The life of humans will not be the same. Death must claim on a massive scale, and I've told you this. Therefore, if you are not a part of the covenant of life, ark of life, the chosen of life; then you will not be saved. Thus, I've told you, billions are going to die. The spirit; that energy inside of you is your true being. Once that being and or, energy, and or, spirit sheds the flesh, then for billions of you, your judgement begins.

If you belong to death and or, are apart of death's world then there is no way you can be saved. Therefore, I've told you in other books; know what your sins are because God and or, Lovey truly do not judge anyone. Our sins we do on a daily basis judge us; are our judgement if we are not forgiven of these sins. And contrary to popular beliefs, and what the agents of death tell you about God forgiving you of your sins, I am here to tell you, and have told you in other books God and or, Lovey cannot forgive you of your sins if that sin is not against Lovey. So, if you wronged and or, erred and or, sinned against your mother, father, sister, brother, sister Pat, brother Elroy; then these people are the ones to forgive you. God cannot step in and forgive you of your sin done to them. If God did this then; God and or, Lovey would and will be overstepping his and her authority. God and or, Lovey would and will be taking your brother's, sister's, mother, father, sister Pat's, brother Elroy's right from them. Therefore, God and or, Lovey would be a liar, and deceiver.

As humans, we have forgotten that the job of the devil, and their children is to get as many of you to hell as possible. Therefore, if your sins outweigh your good, then know for a fact without doubt that; you are going to go to hell; the planet of doom and gloom as I call it to live out the remainder of your spiritual life. If you've read any of my other books, you cannot say that I've not told you; _**"the life you live here on earth determines where you go once the spirit shed the flesh,"**_ because I've told you this time and time again.

I've also told you, _**"life is guaranteed." You are the ones to take life as well as, let other's take life from you.**_ You know that misery loves comfort therefore, because evil and or, evil spirits, love comfort, they will take you to hell with them. But guess what, in hell you are contained in your own jail and or, containment unit therefore, misery lives in misery alone, and so will you. Know that there are no air conditioners in hell, no water just spiritual fire, spiritual fire you created for self due to your actions and or, sins you did and or, do here on earth. God and or, Lovey cannot create your fire for you because you are the one to sin reckless and rude without regard for your life.

You are the ones to run behind religion, and believe in the lies of religion. Read your nasty bible again and see how filthy this book depicts Lovey and or, God.

Read it and see your nasty beginning, and nasty end. Therefore, know that; **MAN'S NASTY BOOK; YOUR SO – CALLED HOLY BIBLE IS <u>DEATH'S BOOK; THE BOOK OF THE DEAD.</u>** Therefore, your God is death. Jesus for some.

You believe in dead profits; whoops prophets.

You praise the dead; your dead profits; whoops prophets. Hence, many of you emulate them; your dead profits; whoops prophets and, carry their nasty legacy with you throughout your life as well as, to your death; grave.

Now let me ask again. **<u>IF YOUR GOD IS DEAD, WHY ARE YOU STILL ALIVE; LIVING?</u>**

Your god is dead, but you are still alive. Does your logic make any sense? And, do not say it does not work that way. It works that way. You follow death and the lies of death therefore, you are going to die. You cannot have spiritual life because, **<u>LOVEY AND OR GOD; THE TRUE AND LIVING GOD KNOWS YOU NOT PERIOD.</u>**

Therefore Lovey, our good and true people must rise up good and true without fear of them; the wicked and evil that will seek to kill us.

We must rise up good and true Lovey, and be shielded, and protected from what is to come.

As your good and true people, we must secure our ark with you now.

We must find our safe haven with you so that; we can live our life in true peace and harmony with you, and without them wanting to come into our lands and infect it with their nastiness.

Global food shortage is coming.

Unclean drinking water is here, and it's only a matter of time where the waters of the globe become undrinkable.
This is why we Lovey have to, and must secure pure and clean drinking water for our children and people before death takes on a massive scale. We need to be truly prepared and ready Lovey.

As Black People, your true and good people, we cannot and, can no longer live as the dead.

We can no longer live is disunity.

We can no longer be crabs in a barrel that is climbing and clawing each other down to get out of that barrel and or, to the top.

We can no longer live under the devil's systems of lies and deceit.

We can no longer live under the law and laws of death.

We must live life good and true; clean. Therefore, it's imperative that you are with us good and true Lovey to show us the way.

It's time for the exodus Lovey, therefore, we must leave out of Babylon and secure our good and true place with you.

Babylon and the different children of Babylon cannot come with us therefore, no unclean beasts, humans, and spirits allowed under any circumstance (s).

Our good and true life is good and true with you Lovey. Therefore, our good and true life must be sealed off without breakage, any form of breakage from the wicked and evil of this world and universe including the spiritual realm. Evil cannot, and must never ever infiltrate our world and community with you, and you with us ever again Lovey. Therefore Lovey, the evil gene that is within us; our body, mind, and spirit **must** be destroyed more than infinitely and indefinitely, never to ever rise again. Evil must never ever gain access to our physical and spiritual DNA ever again.

Lovey, evil must not use sex, music, their unclean ways, technology, and more unclean and evil things to lure us from you ever again come on now.

TRUTH IS EVERLASTING LIFE, AND WE MUST LIVE AS THE TRUTH MORE THAN INDEFINITELY. Therefore, lies, all facet(s) of evil must be truly more than infinitely and indefinitely more than forever ever without end be locked away from us. This I choose for myself Lovey as well as, choose and chose for the good and true seeds you've given me. I cannot let evil in. Therefore, let it be done and let evil go with their wicked and evil own.

Just look at earth and see the destruction of earth.

Look at how humans have and has destroyed this once beautiful planet. Earth has and have become the whore house of death.

Earth has become the home and planet of the dead. Just look at the sins of each human including my sins. I see these things, and have to live in filth; why Lovey?

Why do I have to live in filth like them, and amongst them?

Lovey, why earth?

Why did we not close our garden (vagina) off to wicked and evil men and women?

Oh well, life must live on and go on.

Onwards I go with this book because this book is my dream book. What I see that is happening around the world.

Michelle

Wow it's been a hot minute since I've written a dream book.

Have I been lagging lately when it comes to my writing?

Yes. Been taking a break from all format of writing, and have been consumed with my game play on my tablet. Been thinking a lot and writing in my head; meaning, talking to God and or, Lovey my way. Further, I did not want to bother putting some of my dreams in books. I dream so much that wow.

My early mornings are consumed with dreams. Some I can remember vividly, and some I cannot remember.

Did I dream and see Aretha Franklin again?

Yes

She was not arguing with anyone, but someone said something, and she was agreeing and or, said something to the effect of what the person said. So I truly do not know what is going on in her family life. Meaning, what is happening and or, going to happen to her family she left behind. And to be honest with you people, I cannot concern myself with her family because I truly do not know them. Further, this time around, I did not see her as this beautiful black woman, I saw her as she was before she gave up her flesh. Thin and frail, but she was not frail in my dream. She had spunk. So, I am not going to analyze this dream because I truly do not know how to analyze it.

Anthony Bourdain is haunting me. I truly do not know what is troubling for me when it comes to this man's death. I am not sure if there needs to be closure there with him, but something truly do not sit well with this death for me. It's disturbing for me because, I cannot look at his picture without getting the feeling as if something is truly wrong. His death is not what it seems. Wow, because something is truly not right. I know but I truly do not know. He's not speaking, and I can't get him to speak. Meaning, I do not know how to get him to speak to me. Maybe one day a door will be opened to me where I can speak face to face with the dead. No, I don't want that to happen. Scrap that Lovey because, I have enough trouble seeing the dead when I close my eyes at times and, via my dream world. Some dead a gross looking; void of light and life, and I would not be able to handle them. Yes, some pass me by literally too.

Wow because death surrounds me literally. I so do not know why I have to carry life and death with me in this way Lovey. I know this is supposed to be my dream book, but I have to also talk to you my way in these books.

Did I dream and see Marlon Brando in my dream?

Yes

This dream is long. One continuous dream that had to do with food, old Italian men and women, and this young white boy who had something wrong with his feet. One, if not both of his legs were wooden. We were walking to go to his father's restaurant and or, this eatery and he fell on his behind. I helped him up I believe, and told him about my leg issues, but he was not interested in my leg issues. He just walked ahead of me. Suffice it to say; we ended up in this restaurant. I lost sight of him and the others that was with us. Like I said, Marlon Brando was in the dream because there is more to this dream. What was weird about Marlon

Brando was that he had tube; this tube around his neck area. The tube is a breathing tube for me. So I do not know if there is going to be an outbreak in Italy, or somewhere in the Italian community globally where older Italian men and women get sick if not die.

Prior to this dream though, I was dreaming about older white people as if something is going to happen to the older generation of white people globally. I say globally because, I told you in another book that; it's time for White People based on hue, and based on hue and evil deeds to die. Their wickedness and evil has and have gone on for far too long. The lies of them has and have affected the global community in a negative way. Therefore, they must pay for the lies they preach, teach, as well as, force you to accept.

You cannot say, and write books of lies on life and think you are going to get away with your nasty book and books; your so called holy bible and or, holy books.

You cannot say; God said, *"thou shalt not kill,"* then make God to be a giver backer taker by going back on his word.

What we as humans do not realize is that; **_IF YOUR ARE GIVEN A DIRTY BEGINNING YOUR END CANNOT, AND WILL NEVER EVER BE CLEAN._**

YOU CANNOT GIVE DIRTY AND EXPECT TO BE CLEAN IN THE END. YOU WILL NEVER EVER BE CLEAN, YOU WILL FOREVER BE DIRTY. THEREFORE, I TELL YOU AND WILL FOREVER

TELL YOU. IF THE HEAD IS DIRTY, THEN THE BODY CANNOT, AND WILL NEVER BE CLEAN.

<u>So, if God is dirty; humans cannot be clean. Humans will be dirty also.</u>

If your pastor is dirty, you as the congregation of that church cannot be clean. You are dirty; if not dirtier than your pastor and or, the person that is preaching and or, teaching you.

If you are conceived in sin, you cannot be clean; you are sinful, and your life is sinful. Therefore, it is wise to know who you procreate with because evil do come through the loins of men and women. Yes, there is forgiveness for adultery, but after knowing what adultery is; you will not be forgiven if you continue living an adulterous life. You know the truth therefore, you must live by the truth.

This is the end for the White Race based on hue and hue and evil deeds. You cannot defy Lovey and or, God and think that someone and or, God's children is going to go against Lovey and save you. This will never happen. Good cannot save evil, nor was good commissioned to save evil; the wicked and evil of this earth.

It's amazing how some of you use God to get what you want. God is not a fool hence, the price some of you will and must pay in hell. God did not give any of you unclean doctrines, or seeds to give to humanity. So, truly woe be unto the lots of you for real.

Yes, the Black Race has and have a saving grace, but you've forgotten that not all in the Black Community fall under the Black Banner of Life. Not all Blacks are Blacks therefore, **"life is not governed by the colour and or the complexion of one's skin." "Life is based on the good that you do, and the truth that you uphold and keep."**

Your lies are not truth hence; LIFE MUST TURN FROM YOUR RACE DUE TO YOUR LIES; SPITEFUL AND DECIETFUL WAYS AND NATURE.

In your so called holy book it is written; **"thou shalt not kill"** yet, the politicians and some religious leaders in your country and or, community send people on the battlefield to kill; murder and or dishonour the flesh of another human being. You spill blood on that land, thus causing death to walk in that country and take at will. Therefore, you pollute the earth with your wickedness, lies and deceit. **Therefore, your murder; are murderers that have no respect for life.**

You also tell lies on Lovey, but then again, Lovey was never your choice and stay.

Lovey was not your life and or, a part of your life because you preach and teach death.

You allow death to walk, talk, and take at will therefore, death is your god and true friend.

DEATH IS YOUR BEGINNING, AND DEATH MUST BE YOUR END.

I also dreamt Rihanna. The dream was like a movie; as if she was in a movie, and in the movie she was pregnant and did not know who the father of the child was. In the dream she regretted dating I believe three men. Do not quote me on the three but quote me on two to three men. So, I do not know if she is going to do another movie. I will not analyze this dream because this dream could be layered thus the regrets she had in the dream.

Those dreams I had in the last part and or, last week of September people. No, I've not been keeping a dream journal, nor do I truly want to with some dreams.

It's October 5th, and I am so not going to worry about the English and or, British Monarch.

Dreamt Meghan Markle again. Dreamt, she was getting married again to Harry, and there was a family procession. My family was in the procession but the people and or, family members that were in the procession was not my earthly, and spiritual family. These were her family, and the people were dressed to a tee in beautiful ball gowns. We; some of the black family members were late, not dressed, and we were hurrying to get to where we need to be to get dressed. On our way, Meghan was in this beautiful dress, and she collapsed to the ground. **_She was being poisoned._** I knew what to do in the dream, and this black woman now told this white man how to get rid of poison from the body. I was upset with her because, everything we as black people know; we tell to the white race and dem capitalize pon it, and lef wi inna total poverty. Certain things we as black people do not keep to ourselves and make it benefit us, and this is so sad.

So, the warning is there, and if Meaghan's mother do not take heed then; her daughter, if not her is going to die. Shi a Jamaican and Jamaican's know what I am talking about when it comes to poison in the system; body. We know what to do, and what to use. Therefore, the warning is there, and I am seeing what is happening in this girl's life. But then again, she was the sacrifice from the day she married into this family anyway. Trust me, she's been commissioned for death without her knowing it, and I did tell you what I saw in another book.

<u>Death must be fed and some family you are not to marry into because the roots of them is pure evil.</u> Therefore, the children of death must keep death fed by any means necessary.

So whomever dies in this Monarch is not my concern because; **<u>"LIFE, AND THE TRUE LIONS, LYONS, LYON MUST BE VINDICATED AT ALL COST FOR REAL."</u>**

Judgement!!!!!!!!!!!!!!!!!!!!!

All must come crashing down and will come crashing down for the British Monarch. Trust me, earth is truly not going to be the same once all is said and done. ***Time will tell, and must tell.***

TIME WILL TELL – Bob Marley

Humans; wicked and evil humans and spirit must be destroyed.

I know for a fact without doubt that billions of you have and has a home in hell. Your containment unit awaits and trust me, not one of you will get out.

There is mass destruction coming, I know this because the evils of men; humans have and has gone too far.

Yes, for those who know. Evil has five thousand, nine hundred and ninety-seven more years to wreak havoc on earth, but I am hoping that Lovey will secure his and her own.

Also, I truly hope, and petition Lovey to let this time be over now. Humans did make the choice to follow death, and do the bidding of death. Therefore, I am hoping that all ends before 2032 where evil; all evil is evicted from earth, and the good and true of this earth, universe and beyond can live their life in goodness and in truth more than infinitely and indefinitely, and more than forever ever without end.

The good and true should not live amongst the wicked and evil, nor should the good and true see the wickedness and evils of them. It's not fair for good to be contaminated by those who are truly not of good and true life come on now.

Life isn't about death and conflict.
Life isn't about lies.

Life isn't about heaven and hell. Life is about truth; true truth and goodness, and if you cannot live good and true then you have not life but death; are a part of the realm of death come on now.

It's October 6th, and my dream world is consumed with my game play. The eliminating of things. Been playing too much Farmville as of late, but it cannot be helped. I am trying to get to the diamond league, so I've been truly playing for keeps. Truly love this game. Therefore, I play this game more than my other games.

Hey, I'm progressing in my game play. Need more likes though, but as I progress and build my farm, I am sure and or, hoping to get more likes.

Now with that said and, with my game play affecting my dream world again. I dreamt a country in the Middle East. In the dream I believe the land and or, country was Iran. This news caster; male news caster that was dressed in a dark if not black suit was talking. He showed this shuttle taking off; going up in this residential area of the country. I so do not want to go to Google Images to search the image I need because in truth, I truly do not need anything to do with the Islamic Nations globally period. I truly have a bone to pick with them therefore, they are cursed, and I've cursed them. Not that my curses stick. My curses are weak, weaker than weak therefore, my curses do not doom anyone.

Now with that said; onwards with the dream. A shuttle went up into the sky in a residential area with houses of cream colour, and flat top roofs. The news caster mention something about Islamic Kingdom. I truly cannot remember if war had actually begun. **_War I did not see._** Meaning, a war on the Islamic Kingdom where they were bombed prior to the news caster showing the image of the shuttle going up. But something happened, and this is why the shuttle was sent up. I will not analyze this dream because after seeing that dream; I woke up and wondered what conflict is going to happen in Iran and or, the Middle Eastern countries where war come into play.

Like I said, I truly do not care about the Islamic Nations globally hence my book ***Islamic Thought*** that is available on Lulu.com, and other online retailers. Family and people; my true family. **You cannot say you are OF GOD AND MURDER; KILL. YOU ARE NOT OF LIFE BUT OF DEATH.**

YOU CANNOT SAY ALLAH, AND TAKE LIFE FROM THE BREATH OF LIFE.

YOU ARE NOT OF ALLAH BUT OF DEATH BECAUSE, NOT ONE OF THEM ARE PEACEFUL, NOR DO THEY KNOW WHAT ALLAH STAND FOR, AND REPRESENT.

They are wannabees, and this is why **ALLAH HAS ABSOLUTELY NOTHING TO DO WITH THEM. THEY ARE NOT OF LIFE BUT OF DEATH.** No peace is within them therefore, they speak their father's tongue, and create conflict everywhere they go. *THUS GOD AND OR, LOVEY HAVE ABSOLUTELY NOTHING TO DO WITH BABYLON, AND BABYLONIANS.*

NONE, NOT ONE CAN BE FOUND ON LOVEY'S AND OR, GOD'S MOUNTAIN OF LIFE. THIS YOU CAN QUOTE ME ON WITHOUT DOUBT. I DID NOT SEE ONE BABYLONIAN ON LOVEY'S MOUNTAIN THEREFORE, YOU AS HUMANS MUST KNOW THAT

THE MOUNTAIN OF GOD AND OR, LOVEY IS VITAL. Yes, some see the tree of life, therefore, trees and mountains are valuable to life here on earth. Therefore, know your tree and mountain of life. This is why I also petition Lovey to take the White Race based on hue and based on hue and evil deeds off his and her mountain of life. Dem too dyam wicked and evil. They, the White Race have and has no respect for life. Therefore, they live to hate and create strife. Yes, I've told you some whites based on hue are black, but I am tired of them now. Tried of the shit they do in life and or, here on earth and get away with it. Well not for long anyway given what I've seen, and seeing now.

Let me tell you this people including my true family and people. **LIFE CANNOT BE SUPERIOR TO LIFE.**

THE WHITE RACE IS NOT SUPERIOR TO THE BLACK RACE BECAUSE NOTHING ON THIS PLANET OR, IN UNIVERSE THE WHITE RACE BASED ON HUE CREATED.

BLACKS CREATED IT ALL THEREFORE, EVERY CULTURE AND OR, RACE BASED ON MAN'S TERMINOLOGY OF RACE HAS AND HAVE STOLEN THE BLACK MAN'S CULTURE, AND SAY IT'S THEIRS.

The FOUNDATION OF LIFE IS BLACK therefore, we all have Black in us. You cannot comprehend, or over stand the true Black Race, and this is why you hate us.

Family hating family and creating strife. *THEREFORE, LOVEY HAS HIS AND HER OWN RACE OF PEOPLE, AND THE DEVIL HAS HIS AND HER OWN RACE OF PEOPLE.*

Yes, it's time for the true Black Race to get ready because evil will not stop creating war and strife on this planet. We as humans are the cause of this because of choice, who we love and not truly love, who we put our trust in, who we chose to lead us via politics, religion, family, tradition wise, and so much more.

No one can put their life above God and or, Lovey but humans do anyway.

Life is not cherished therefore, we have children in sin, live in sin, die in sin, only to go to hell and die. Billions cannot live up or live on because of choice, and this is so sad. Life isn't about death, it's about life. Therefore, the bible of man lie on God. Said, God put strive between his seed and the devil's seed. **<u>God would never ever do this because God and or, Life; Lovey is not a warmonger. Man and or, humans create strife amongst each other.</u>**

Life; good and true life is harmonious and peaceful. Therefore, Lovey and or, God has absolutely nothing to do with the devil's children and people.

Michelle

I so do not know what to tell you Lovey because something is truly not right in North America. My sleep was not a peaceful, or restful sleep. Lovey, why did White People based on hue, and based on wicked and evil deeds mess up this earth, and the lives of everyone here on earth?

Why are they so evil that life truly means nothing to them?

I know something bad is going to happen to North America. It's just a matter of when. This great divide that is coming that I feel. I do not know if the lands are going to literally split apart, or if this divide will do with the new agreement Canada was bullied into signing. <u>Now I am dreaming about this agreement that truly do not sit well in the spiritual realm with this White Man.</u> I truly do not know him, but this agreement truly do not sit well with him. *Yes, he was a man of wealth, and this new agreement that was reached between the United States, Mexico, and Canada <u>affected him; his wealth.</u>* He too did not like the way in which Canada was bullied into signing this agreement. I was telling him when Canada did this; was bullied into signing this new agreement, **<u>it showed how weak Canada was. He also agreed with me on this weakness on Canada's part.</u>**

Lovey, I also stated again, I did not want to stay here in North America, nor do I want my body; flesh to be housed here once my spirit shed the flesh. Lovey, this is my true desire yet; you and those in the spiritual realm is truly not listening to me, and heeding my true desire and need. I truly do not want or need my flesh to be buried here Lovey, and you truly know this. *Something bad is going to happen in North America. War is coming because all this President, the President of the United States is doing is create strife for war to start. He is* a warmonger therefore, what he is doing is not sitting well and right in the spiritual realm.

Lovey, why am I still here in North America against my good and true will?

Lovey, why do these people; the White Race based on hue, and based on hue and evil deeds love to accommodate evil; war?

Why are they so evil and vile?

<u>Why is it that Americans cannot live in true peace with anyone?</u>

You cannot create strife with others and expect to live in true peace come on now Lovey. America facilitate death, and you Lovey know this yet, the land and people are truly not being punished for the wrongs and evils that they do. Why keep this land going Lovey when you know the evils they do each and every day?

You deemed Jamaica unclean; dirty yet, modern day Israel; America is not deemed unclean; dirty why?

Is this land not like Sodom and Gomorrah; the land of whoredom, fornication, murder, all that is wicked and evil also?
Does Satan not have his true home in this land also?

So, why keep this land going?

Are you not ashamed of the way in which the government of the land treat the Black People of the land? Yes, your people reside in that land; America, but in truth: <u>ARE THEY; THESE PEOPLE TRULY YOUR PEOPLE?</u>

<u>Do they; your people not abide under the law and rule of the true devils?</u>

<u>DEVILS THAT HAVE THEIR NEW WORLD ORDER OF SIN AND HATE; STRIFE.</u>

Tell me Lovey, what good is America; North America to life when strife is the aim of the United States of America?

<u>CAN PEACE AND TRUE PEACE BE ACHIEVED WHEN ONE BULLIES ALL GLOBALLY?</u>

I live in North America, and I truly want and need to leave this land in peace and true peace. So, why are you not finding a new home for me in goodness and in truth Lovey?

<u>Do you and my life not matter in all of this?</u>

It's time for the truth to reign, and it's time for the White Race to be truly punished globally because, **<u>war and strife is their true aim and goal.</u>** <u>These people are true warmongers.</u> Thus they lied on you about you putting strife between your seed; children, and the devil's seed; children. The lie is great Lovey therefore, you cannot forgive them for the atrocities they have done come on now.

When did lies take precedence over good Lovey?

Yes, the White Man in the spiritual realm did not like how Canada was bullied into signing an agreement with thieves; the unjust. So because of this; the economies of the globe must collapse.

Maybe this is what he was trying to tell me. His wealth was affected by the new trade deal between Canada, Mexico, and the United States and because of this deal, and Canada's weakness; there is going to be an economic crisis where the wealthy see their wealth depleting. I know you know this new deal between the three parties was not the right deal for Canada and the people of Canada. Now, Canadians must pay the price for the weakness and stupidity of their government.

Oh well, such is life Lovey for the greedy, greedy rich globally. Therefore, I told you, we cannot have an American Bank Accounts because I truly do not want, or need to keep their money beyond 90 days.

We need to fund our own currency, and good economy Lovey come on now. And to be fully clear without a shadow of a doubt Lovey, you are my truth and the policies; political policies of men; the different countries globally truly do not concern me. The politics of man is the politics of man. Yes, I see the mess political leaders get their land and people in, and I truly do not care. As long as their policies, and politics do not affect us Lovey then I am truly good to go.

Humans can kick rocks, and chuck when it comes to their unfair and unjust political systems of bribe, thievery, evil, murder, and death.

Michelle
October 2018

Please note, my dreams are all over the place in this book. Meaning, some of these dream are from September of 2018 and earlier. Some dreams; I write on paper, and waited until a later date before I make a book. I know this is laziness on my part because I get so many different dreams, but it cannot be helped. I do need that extra push at times, but I truly do not have that extra push.

Is there more darkness in my room at nights lately?

Yes, to the point where I need a night light to see. One night; I had to leave the light in the washroom on because I knew, and know there were spirits in my room.

Is my sleeping on track as of late?

No, I am back to not sleeping well. I do not know if it's the weather, but my sleep is so off, and the darkness in my room as of late is truly not helping matters for me. Hey, this is my life. I have to contend with spiritual evil, and the forces of evil.

Weird for me I know, but this is life. It cannot be helped.

Have I been seeing children's faces?

Yes, but I will not let these faces worry me. Death must show me death sometimes, and I truly do not know why death has to do this. No, this is a lie. I have life and death with me, as well as, know life and death. I have to see both realms.

Just yesterday, October 21, 2018, I saw this child laying face down in a bathtub, and the mother came and took

the child out of the water. So, I truly do not know which child is going to die in a bathtub. Like I've said time and time again, I truly do not know what waking state visions mean.

There is one particular short story I so want and need to finish, and hopefully I finish it in 2019 and upload it on Lulu.com.

As for my dreams, here we go with more of them.

Michelle

MY WORLD OF DREAMS 2018 – BOOK FIVE

Lovey my dreams; these two dreams are gnawing at me therefore, let me write them down.

Dreamt Kim Fields that she died, and it hurt me. I so can't remember, but I believe I began to cry and said, "what is her mother going to do?"

In the dream, someone else died but it wasn't the chubby one that was in the show. So Charlotte Rae died, for which she recently died, then Kim Fields and someone else died.

I am not going to analyze this dream because I truly do not know what it means. I truly need to leave this dream alone. It does not concern me, nor do I want or need this dream to concern me.

I also dreamt Steven Spielberg. This tall white man went into his bedroom. I would peg this not too short but medium built white man that had a nice body to be in his late to early thirties. Not older but could be but not in my eyes. He went into Steven Spielberg's room; bedroom, and I think turned on the television. I can't remember if he was searching the place, but he was doing something.

Oh man, I can't remember if I said; "what are you doing," or something to that effect. But in Steven's room he had this huge green dresser. The dresser was so simple that it looked poor for this man's standard of life; meaning, money.

I went into the room; bedroom of Steven Spielberg for which he was in there. He had a pleasant smile on his face, and his hair was gray black. His television was on, and he wanted to watch YouTube. So, I went to touch the television screen for YouTube to come on, but nothing happened. His television was old, and the screen was black and showing grains and or, snow, and or, white dots. Think television before flat screen were introduced. *(Hey, maybe they are going to have touch screen tv's where you touch the screen to turn them on real soon. Who knows.)*

Oh man, I am missing something. Our fingers; I believe thumb touched, and his nail was a bit long for a man. Nonetheless, after touching the screen of the television, and it did not work, I went to sit beside him on the sofa that was unkept because it had a throw over it. A blue and white floral throw; dark blue to black floral throw. Like I said, the sofa was unkept. Steven was lying in the sofa, and the room was a bit messy for my liking. Thus, in the dream he looked poor, and his surroundings; home and furniture was old and poor looking. Sitting beside Steven he said; he did not have Google. I tried pulling him up out of the sofa and said something to him pertaining to; "you are rich, and you know people, let's go call the owners of Google."

I can't remember what happened after that. No, nothing happened. The frame of the dream changed, and I went somewhere and came back, and Steven Spielberg's wife was sitting beside him. She looked sick. Her hair was so thin and gray. I can't remember if I wanted to play in Steven's hair and or, comb it, but I said to his wife; "can I brush your hair?" She gladly and quickly gave me the brush to brush her hair.

Lovey, family, and people. Steven's wife's hair was so thin that when I was brushing her hair, you could see her scalp, and this small circular brown patch on her scalp. I told her if I was hurting her to let me know because of the large patch of scalp that was on her head to the way her hair was. Thus to me, she was sickly in the dream.

After brushing her hair, we were some place else. At an event and or, gathering. She, Stevens wife looked good now. Her hair came back and was a nice light pink that was cut nice to the nape of her neck. She was also dressed in light pink and so was I. There was a table to the right of us that had a pinky red table cloth on it for which I straightened out. We were matching in our pink outfits and looked good. After straightening the table cloth we began to walk. Walking, we passed shoe stores, beautiful ladies shoes that were expensive. I thought we were going to go shopping but we didn't. We were now separated, and I was in this field walking in tall green grass and one that looked like J. Boog and or, J. Boogie (Polynesian singer) was picking up sticks, fire sticks and it came to me and or, it was said to me, *"take care of your self today because tomorrow is not guaranteed and or, tomorrow maybe too late."*

So in all I do, I have to take care of myself today and not wait until the next day.

Do I know what this dream mean?

Yes

There are so many variables in this dream, but the clear message is; "we have to take care of ourselves now, and not put off what concerns us, or give us trouble in life family wise, divorce wise, marriage wise, technology wise, financially wise, health wise, until it's too late."

I know what the shoes mean as well. But know Steven's wife's illness could be his illness. For me, wife usually mean husband in my dream world. Therefore, sometimes my dreams do not walk straight. So wife and husband better pay a visit to the doctor and do a thorough check up for cancer and or, other sickness.

Am I missing something?

Yes

I am not 100% sure, but I believe at some point in the dream I said, we are all Canadians here. So I would extend this dream to James Cameron as well.

Sickness is not good and, sickness can cause you to lose it all. I know this for a fact first hand, and without a shadow of a doubt.

Oh man, I forgot. I managed to get Steven Spielberg off the sofa to walk. This was before his wife was sitting beside him. He was crouched down walking. And think of ET touching the little boys fingers when you think of Steven and me touching fingers.

In the dream it also came to me that; ***"HAVING A BLACK CHILD THROUGH ADOPTION GIVES YOU AS A WHITE PERSON BASED ON HUE, NO GUARANTEE THAT IN THE END OF YOUR STAY HERE ON EARTH, AND YOU MOVE ON TO THE SPIRITUAL REALM THAT YOU WILL BE SAVED."***

SO, A BLACK CHILD; (Black Jesus for some) CANNOT SAVE YOU IN THE WHITE RACE when it's all said and done.

YOU CANNOT DO TO GET. Meaning, for those of you in the white race who have adopted black children thinking these black children can and will save you, "IT WILL NOT HAPPEN."

NO CHILD WHETHER LIVING OR DEAD IS GUARANTEED TO SAVE YOU AS A PARENT.

NO SAVING GRACE YOU ARE GUARANTEED.

Check your life, your past, ancestors past, that child's past, that child's ancestors past, your sins, and so much more.

So, when many of us/you think you are saved and or, guaranteed a place with God and or, Lovey, you are truly not guaranteed at all.

Your Jesus bank has and have been closed indefinitely, and rightfully so.

You cannot hate Black People, and expect a Black Child to save you and or, is going to save you.

You cannot treat Black People unfair; poorly and expect a Black Child to save you and or, is going to save you.

YOU DID WRONG THEREFORE, YOU CANNOT GET RIGHT PERIOD.

Michelle
September 2018 and October 2018

Lovey, how do we have a guaranteed place with you?
How do we safeguard this place with you?

How do we safeguard our self with self?

Life is so different with me yet, when I look around at times, I am disappointed with the way humans are living.

What kind of life are we living Lovey?

Wow

Michelle
September 17, 2018

Life is so weird
Life is strange

Life is truly different
It's a different world
Different life we are living

The mindset of people is different
Strange

Altered state
Altered mind
False beginning
False ending
All a part of human life

Michelle
September 17, 2018

Life can be truly good and beautiful
Life can be truly strange

Life is for you
Life is for me

How we live our life is truly up to you.

Michelle
September 17, 2018

I cannot deal for you
Nor, can I deal for me

Life is truly great, but the way we live our life is truly up to you.

Life cannot be tallied.
Life cannot end.

Where good and true life begins is truly up to you.

Truth cannot end
Therefore, good and true life cannot end

In life, you determine if you live or die.

You determine you; all about you whether good or bad.

Michelle
September 17, 2018

So in all we do, those who are banking on a Black Child and or, Black Jesus to save them, will truly not be saved.

Those so called White Jews that are banking on a Black Child and or, Black Jesus to save them will truly not be saved.

So yes, the Jesus and or, Black Bank is closed for billions and rightfully so.

So to the WHITE JEWS THAT KNOW OF THE BLACK SAVING GRACE WHEN IT COMES TO A BLACK CHILD SAVING HUMANITY, *YOU WILL NOT BE SAVED PERIOD. THAT SAVING GRACE HAS AND HAVE BEEN TAKEN FROM THE LOTS OF YOU AND RIGHTFULLY SO.*

It makes no sense to try because in life; ABSOLUTELY NO ONE CAN DO TO GET WHEN IT COMES TO GOD AND OR, LOVEY, AND LOVEY'S CHILDREN AND PEOPLE.

LIFE WAS AND IS GIVEN TO ALL, AND WHEN YOU TAKE LIFE FROM LIFE AND TELL LIES ON LIFE, THEN TRULY DO NOT EXPECT TO BE SAVED IN LIFE, OR BY LIFE.

LIES CANNOT AND WILL NEVER SAVE YOU, ONLY THE TRUTH CAN. SO YES, IT MATTERS NOT WHO YOU KNOW, AND WHAT YOU DO,

WHEN YOU TAKE LIFE FROM LIFE, YOU CANNOT, AND WILL NEVER EVER BE SAVED.

Yes, religion is a lie, and no religion globally will or can save anyone. Think of lies; the atrocities that people do in the name of religion.

Think of the sins people do in the name of religion.

Think of the confusion religion gives.

Think of the double standard of life we as humans live in.

Think of the unfair and unjust law and laws of men that the wicked and evil enact.

Now tell me, why is it that soldiers and police officers do not go to jail and or, prison for their murderous acts?

Tell me, why is it that the ordinary man and or, citizen goes to jail for the crimes they do, (killings) yet, a soldier and police officer cannot, and do not go to jail for killing another human being, and it matters not if the killing is in another country; foreign land?

"THOU SHALT NOT KILL," yet some kill, **are paid to kill; paid assassins that walk the earth free from the crimes they have done unto others.** Now tell me, **are we as humans living just and fair? One is paid to kill, and is deemed a hero for murdering others, yet others; ordinary citizens as they are called, have to face long prison terms and or, sentences.** So yes, humans live by double standards without knowing they are fools; fooling self into thinking with all the lies they tell and accept; the double standard they live by, they are going to be saved when they are truly not going to be saved in the end. Hell will be their home for a time for some, and time times time for some due to sin.

Therefore, **there cannot be justice in an unjust world.** Meaning, if humans write and live by unjust law and laws, how can they fully and truly have a good and true life?

You cannot live by the laws of death and think you will have life once your spirit shed the flesh.

You cannot live by the law and laws of death and think you are living life. You are not living life, you are doing all to please death; die.

You cannot go against life and think that life will save you, send you a saving grace in the end.

Yes the foundation of life is black, and God's and or, Lovey's children are Black with nappy and or, kinky hair, but not all black that have nappy and or, kinky hair fall under the Black Banner of Life. Some blacks are white and yes, some whites are Black hence God and or, Lovey truly do not look at skin tone when it comes to people globally. Therefore, I tell you and will forever tell you: "THE LIFE YOU LIVE HERE ON EARTH, DETERMINE WHERE YOU GO ONCE YOUR SPIRIT SHED THE FLESH."

Think and be wise because as it is, billions of you here on earth have "NO SAVING GRACE." THUS, "BILLIONS OF YOU

ARE SLATED TO DIE." Meaning, your name is in Death's book.

And yes, this is why many of you worship and praise the dead via rites and customs, religion, traditions of men, so called family traditions, acceptance of other people's culture without knowing your own roots and culture, marriage, death, and so much more.

LIFE CANNOT BE DEATH.

DEATH IS DEATH, and billions of you truly do not know this.

Yes, the Steven Spielberg's dream is layered, but as Revelations said in your so called holy book. *"WOE BE UNTO THE JEWS THAT CALL THEMSELVES JEWS BECAUSE THEY ARE OF THE <u>SYNAGOGUE</u> OF SATAN."*

Until this day some of you cannot put this together. Thus the devil has their seed of people, and life has their true and righteous people that must go up to life; see Lovey when all is said and done. *Therefore, I've told you about the upright and downward triangle in different books. I told you the difference between the two and what you should not do.*

Therefore, <u>**know life and death.**</u>

<u>**Know where you stand in life**</u> because; the life you live here on earth, determines where you go once the spirit shed the flesh, and I've told you this above as well as in other books. Your religious leaders cannot save you. <u>**Only you can save you**</u> because; no clergyman, woman or child can

forgive you of sins and or, wrongs you have done to someone else. So if you wronged your next-door neighbour, it is your next-door neighbour you must go to for forgiveness. Your clergy saying do how many hail Mary's cannot forgive you of that sin. **_Your sin is still on your sin record._**

Your clergy saying go to God for forgiveness cannot save you. God cannot forgive you for your sins done unto others.

You sinned against your brother, it is your brother that must forgive you. Yes it's good to ask God for forgiveness which is fine, do not stop doing this, but know that God cannot forgive of sins that is not done unto him and her. If God forgave you of your sin with your brother and others, then God would be taking the right of the person you sinned from them, and God and or, Lovey would never do that, break his and her own law and laws of life.

As humans you need to know that the devil need to keep your name in the book of death, hence misery love comfort. Meaning, the more you sin and follow death, is the longer your stay in hell if your sin and sins are not forgiven. So if you have more sins on your sin record than good on your good record, truly do not look for a saving grace because you cannot and will not be saved. Yes, your child can save you if that child is good; given a saving grace, but truly do not bank on your child to save you if you do not have a good and true relationship with that child. Therefore, not all children are given a saving grace due to sin, the sins of the fathers, mothers, ancestors of old. So, **_every so called WHITE JEW, MUST LOOK AT THEIR PAST, AND THE PAST OF THEIR ANCESTORS._** This is also what the Steven Spielberg's dream was telling me. They, the so called WHITE JEWS know the lies they told in man's so called holy book; bible. *Therefore, the Black Race cannot save them; the so called White Jews because they did write the BOOK OF DEATH WHICH IS MAN'S SO CALLED HOLY BIBLE.*

- ✓ ***THEY DID LIE ON GOD.***
- ✓ ***THEY DID SELL OUT GOD.***
- ✓ ***THEY DID ACCEPT THE BABYLONIAN WAY OF LIFE.***

Therefore, to me and for me, the dry sticks J. Boogie was picking up, represents them, and the hell they are going to face once their spirit shed the flesh. So yes, I am seeing the HELL THE SO-CALLED WHITE JEWS MUST FACE.

Family and people; my true family; tell me, what did Lovey do to these people for them to lie on Lovey so?
What did Lovey do to them for them to hate and despise Lovey so?

You lied on God who you claim to be your God and or, father. But God was never your stay and father, hence you said; Abraham a known Babylonian, a family ram, and idol worshipper that practiced animal and human sacrifices as your father.

Abraham made sacrifices unto the devil and this is documented in your so-called holy bible. Melchezidec was truly not of God. Therefore, God and or, Lovey truly do not deal in money; materialistic possessions, and the riches; wealth of humans because Lovey did give his and her people all the wealth they needed. Thus, all the WEALTH OF THE EARTH CAN BE FOUND IN BLACK LANDS.

Man's beginning here on earth is based on nastiness therefore, man's end here on earth cannot be clean. Humans must die and or, end nasty. Therefore, I will forever tell you, "if the head is dirty, the body cannot be clean." Your body will never be clean if; _**you accept and are given a filthy and nasty beginning.**_

Life cannot and will never be extended to you because you are not clean. Plus good luck to you on getting your name out of the BOOK OF DEATH if your name is in it. So, know your life and death here on earth.

For you the true Black Race, I am going to give you "CHANGES" by Tupac despite his behaviour in the physical realm, and the life he lived and participated in here on earth. Listen to the words and or, the lyrics of the song. _**Hear when he said; "take the evil out the people, they'll be acting right."**_ *We need to change ourselves and the community we live in for the better; our betterment if we are to survive what is to come shortly.*

**You are the truth; stop letting other nations including our own degrade you and your identity; truth.**

Onwards I go with more dreams.

Michelle
October 2018

Wow Lovey because I truly don't know what the people in this world is coming to.

How do you ascertain life Lovey?

This dream I just had that was so brutal.

Lovey, it's September 23, 2018 and I dreamt this newscaster; male newscaster talking but could not be seen. He was showing a video that went viral on the internet of Neo Nazi's beating; brutally beating a civilian, and then brutally beating a Scottish Police Officer in riot gear.

Lovey, in the dream they were in this place with tables. The civilian who was dressed in a white tank top – tank top looking top and blue jeans tried to get away but could not. She was on the table and was kicked off to the ground. Then they kicked the civilian and began to spit on the civilian. I did not see the civilian's face, but I would assume the civilian was female from her attire and shape. After that happened, some of the Neo Nazi's who was a part of Scotland's finest *(police force)* turned on their own police officers. One specifically that caught my eye. The Neo Nazi's began to use their baton to beat them; the other officers who were not Neo Nazi's. One of the attackers facial covering was pulled off, and she was a female with very curly red hair, and straight nose. She was skinny also. I could not watch anymore. As the newscaster said, the video went viral on the internet of the attack. So, truly thank you Lovey for letting me want to use the washroom in real life because seeing what I saw was truly disturbing in the dream. Too brutal for me to the attack. Also, in the dream, the Neo Nazi's had this black mark on their hand. Left hand from my positioning. Now Lovey tell me; what's going on in Scotland especially in their police force?

Is Scotland going to be attacked?

Are there Neo Nazi's in the Scottish police force that no one knows about?

Wow Lovey because this dream is so not nice.

Michelle

Now, let me ask you this Lovey.

Is there a place in your world and kingdom for the spiteful and hateful?

Is there a place in your world and kingdom for Neo Nazi's?

Yes, I know that was a dumb and stupid question, but Lovey; why do people hate others so much?

Do they not know that all they fight against is in them?

Lovey; "THE FOUNDATION OF LIFE IS BLACK," therefore, every individual on this planet whether race, colour, lineage, or creed has and have "BLACK" in them. No one can get away from this because **_there is no such thing as pure blood, or pure race._**

Humans; some humans are just spiteful and hateful. You fight and kill your brother for something that is in you.

Lovey, do these Neo Nazi's make any sense?

THEREFORE, "BRAINWASHED FOOLS, WILL ALWAYS ACT LIKE FOOLS."

Lovey, wrong and false education is a bitch in life. Therefore, Bob Marley specifically told us not to let them "school" us. The school systems of men only graduate "thieves and murderers," and he Bob Marley was infinitely, and indefinitely correct. He also said; _"man to man is so unjust, you do not know who to trust,"_ and he is correct with those words also.

Therefore, "Babylon System; "the White Man's System is a "vampire" sucking the life and blood of their victims; which are humans; globally each and every day. No wonder they killed Bob Marley. He knew too much and was calling out the evil systems of men; humans globally.

VAMPIRE – Peter Tosh

Michelle
September 23, 2018

Now tell me Lovey; **how can you look upon a race and people that rape and brutalize the different races and generations of life?**

How can you Lovey have mercy upon the merciless?

Look at them; the White Race Lovey and tell me if this is what life is all about given their behaviour; vile and lying nature?

Humans suffered and died because of them; the White Race?

They the White Race based on hue and evil deeds did rape life of life in all; yet, **you still have this sick and demented race on your mountain; why?**

Look at how earth has become run down – a cesspool of filth; sin because of them; their lies and deceit.

Look at how earth is being ruined by them and others. Now tell me, **what did earth do for you to turn your back on her in this way when it comes to the vile nature of man; humans?**

Yes, I know evil is contained here on earth, but Lovey; man; humans want to spread their vile ways in the sky; their so-called universe. I say so called because the sky is not the universe, but the sky.

SO LOVEY, WHAT DO YOU SEE WHEN YOU LOOK AT THEM; WHITE PEOPLE BASED ON HUE, AND BASED ON HUE AND EVIL DEEDS?

DO YOU HOLD YOUR HEAD DOWN IN SHAME AND DISGRACE BECAUSE OF THEM?

LOVEY, THIS IS SCOTLAND; THE LAND OF MY ANCESTORS. PLEASE DO NOT LET SCOTLAND BECOME VILE AS THE LAND OF MY BIRTH; JAMAICA.

LET EVIL LEAVE SCOTLAND ALONE.

Michelle
September 23, 2018

Oh man, my dates are incorrect. Today is the 23rd, not the 22nd, or the 21st, of September.

Lovey, how can humans be so cold and heartless?

Lovey, man; humans are living so vile and wicked; without mercy yet, they want a saving grace from you.

Are humans that naïve that they would think you would save the sinful and merciless?

Lovey fi real. **Do humans not think of their fire pit in hell?**

Have humans truly forgotten about hell and the fire that is going to consume their spirit?

Lovey wow.

Yes, hell is happy to receive the spirit of humans. It's just humans that cannot see what awaits them when the spirit shed the flesh for real.

Lovey, all these people who live for hate, live to spread hate, live to kill, live to threaten and bully, and more evil things. **Do they not think of their life when the get old especially when they die?** Therefore, I see death before me. I also see hell, know the fire of hell that consumes the spirit Lovey, **so why are humans living to die instead of living to live?**

Why take up the cross and crosses of death if you don't have to?

Why follow others? Let other's brainwash you to become hateful and spiteful?

Why go to hell to die alongside them?

Is your life not worth something?
Do you not value your life?

Michelle
September 23, 2018

Aye Lovey, thank you for not making me a part of the White Race of Death, Lies, Dishonesty; Sin, and so much more evil things.

Truly thank you for making me a part of the goodness of life.

Truly thank you for making me truly ***"BLACK LIKE YOU,"*** with beautiful natural hair that differentiate me from the rest of the global community; population.

Truly thank you for giving me hope, truth, true goodness, true truth, true life; you.

I know life is coming to an end here on earth for billions because the fighting is truly not over yet. But Lovey, let it be done. Meaning, let your good and true people escape the fighting and judgement that is brewing in the heavens; the planet of doom and gloom as I call this world.

Lovey, why let earth continue to house evil when you and I know that all facets of evil can be stopped?

Why let death including spiritual death walk amongst the living?

Lovey, it's time to separate truth from lies; myths and fiction. Lovey, our good and true people must separate from death's people now. It's time for all evil empires, land (s), people, farmers, water, but water is not evil so exclude water to be punished, and be no more, more than infinitely and indefinitely; more than forever ever without end.

So Lovey, truly separate our good and true, and truly trying to be good from all that is wicked and evil right now. Let evil go with their true own Lovey. And Lovey, just to add a footnote and note, although the waters of life is truly not evil but, the water that keep the wicked and evil nourished cannot be the same water that nourish and feed the good and true, and truly trying to be good. Lovey, everything that is of ours must, and should stay more than forever ever without end from the evil, wicked and evil and sinful of this world. Separation, separation, separation.

Good can no longer be integrated with evil come on now. We are defeating the purpose as well as defeating life when we continue to harbour and live amongst, side by side, and nearby evil come on now.

Therefore Lovey, you must forever ever without end say no to integration, and infinitely and indefinitely yes to separation and or, segregation. Good can no longer mingle with, or live with, or amongst evil of any kind.

Michelle

Lovey, why are humans so evil and corrupt globally?

Why do we as humans let others; other humans put us in dangerous positions?

Why do we allow them; evil humans to corrupt and manipulate us with their lies and hate?

Why do we allow these evil people to educate us as well as, build systems of hate and confusion to take us from physical and spiritual life?

LOVEY, WHEN DID GOOD AND TRUE LIFE BECOME HATE; THE VICTIM OF THE UNCLEAN?

Lovey, can anyone measure life?

Can anyone tell what life is worth?

Can anyone put a value on life; good and true life?

So Lovey, if you know not life; how can you have life, or know what life is worth?

Your life is not a trip to the doctor, medicine man or woman, or a trip to the grocery store; your life is a trip to you. Meaning, you need to know you, your worth and or, value in life, your life because absolutely no one can live your life for you. You cannot be replaced therefore; true life is absolute. Your life depends on you and how you live it. Therefore, know you and the life you carry with you. Your flesh is not life. Your spirit is. However; your flesh reflect the spirit; is a reflection of the spirit; your identical you. You spirit can live without the flesh, and your spirit can live without your identical you.

Therefore, higher life and higher learning. True knowledge is key and or, one of the keys to true, pure, and everlasting life.

Michelle
September 23, 2018

Lovey what is going to happen in Africa and or, Jamaica?

Yesterday while in the kitchen I saw these colours in the base heater of my apartment. I have never seen bright colours in a heater before. I never thought of it, nor did I make what I saw concern me because yesterday, with yesterday being October 14th, 2018 bother me until now. Lovey I truly don't know but I know.

I know I am not going crazy. This is time for more darkness and or, darkness. Lately, my room has become darker than normal, and I know someone is in my room. Sometimes I feel a female presence. It's scary but not so scary because I refuse to let these spirits scare me.

Do I need a vacation?

Yes

As for the colours I saw in the heater I have to ask again; what is going to happen in Africa and or, Jamaica?

Jamaican Rastas wear and or, rock, and or, rep the colours I saw in my base heater.

Africa and or, Africans wear and or, rock, and or, rep the colours I saw in my base heater. So what's going to happen to Black People globally Lovey?

Are the true BLACKS of the globe going to truly find their way home?

Is further violence going to erupt in Africa where we see Blacks killing each other more?

Is a heatwave or volcano going to erupt in Africa sending lava on land?

Lovey, I truly do not know because I fully and truly do not understand, comprehend, or over stand waking state visions. I just have to leave well enough alone and see what happens.

Lovey, I have to add this also. Is something horrible going to happen to the gay community in Canada and or, globally? They too rock some of the colours I saw in the base heater.

Michelle
October 15, 2018

Given what I saw Lovey, I have to ask you this now. Are you pleased with the Black Race based on hue with the exclusion of all Babylonians, and the Whites that/who fall under the Black Banner of life?

<u>Are you not disgusted and ashamed of the way Blacks are killing Blacks?</u>

<u>Are you not disgusted and ashamed of the way Blacks disgrace self?</u>

<u>Are you not disgusted and ashamed of the way we are living?</u>

We are not unified Lovey, and this is so disturbing to me.

Aye Lovey, DON'T BLAME LIFE by Bugle.

Do you hold your head down in shame and disgrace to see what we have become, and how far we as a people have and has fallen from grace?

Lovey, you've tried so hard with us to have us; many in the Black Race based on hue and given the exclusions above disgrace and dishonour you.

Lovey, how can you save us when we in the Black Race cry wolf, and play the victim all the time. Meaning, when you send good and true people to educate and teach us the truth, we are the same ones to set these people up for death.

So now Lovey, how can you save the unsaved; ones that say they need a saving grace but deep down truly do not want or need to be saved? They are disgruntled, yet do nothing to lift self out of mental slavery, physical and spiritual slavery; bondage.

Lovey, you cannot use the devil's book to teach clean come on now.

We say we are Blacks yet, teach from the devil's book. No one can teach you about life from the devil's and or, death's book come on now. Yes, we all have and or, billions of us has and have the devil's book in our home. That's fine, but what kind of life can you teach from a dirty book?

Yes, I refer back to the book of death, but Lovey, why do we still have this book in our possession. Let me know later what to do because right now Lovey, I truly do not know what to do given my waking state vision with those colours in my base board heater.

Michelle
October 2018

Wow Lovey what's going on? This is such a weird dream that I had just now.

Dreamt Richard Gere the white actor. He had black hair and dark glasses on. He was being brought up before congress, but he was not in the congressional building but outside, and Matthew Perry was in the crowd; huge crowd of people.

In the dream, Richard Gere and Roman Polansky were brought up for and or, on charges for sleeping with minors – male boys. They were apart of a sex ring; huge sex ring where they violated, and slept with young boys.

Matthew Perry was somehow at my side now, and I said to him; "why don't you run for Mayor of Toronto, I would help him. He would be the first person I helped, but he said no, he wants to run things his way, and not let people tell him how to run his office and or, Toronto." He did not get to elaborate on what he meant because all of a sudden, this spaceship came out of the sky and dropped cans. I think three cans. I thought it was beer. Matthew ran to the ship when it came down, got a can, and said; "Red Bull gives you wings." The can was big, and you could see the blackish can. I believe the can was open, no, I believe he opened the can and said; Red Bull gives you wings. You could see the writing on the can. Therefore, to me, and in the dream Matthew was doing a Red Bull commercial.

Oh man, I can't remember if there were tall grayish buildings in the background of Matthew when he said those words. Also, in the dream I knew what Matthew Perry meant when he said he did not want anyone to tell him how to run and or, govern Toronto. People think politicians do things on their own but don't. They have to, meaning, _**politicians have to take orders from higher up. They, the elected do not run the country. Hence they are a front for the more powerful that is above them.**_

Michelle
September 13, 2018

After all that I saw with Richard Gere and Matthew Perry, I was in beautiful Nova Scotia sight seeing. I can't tell you this dream people because it's so different. It involved Russians, food, this eatery, hotel, and how this place was a part of Nova Scotian history.

In the dream, the hotel eatery had juke boxes that still played, and this old Russian owner giving tours of the place.

Let me stop because I am telling you the dream.

Wow, these two men that was sitting in a room. One had on this different looking suit that had gold and or, gold printing on it. He had a upright cross, and an inverted cross in his ear. He said nothing. He was just sitting there with another man. So Lovey tell me this; how can death be two ways?

Never mind, he was physical and spiritual death. Now let me ask you this; is physical and spiritual death going to hit Nova Scotia and or, Russia real soon?

I know death is claiming and, death is truly not done. But is Nova Scotia and Russia on the hit list and or, target list for death in a brutal way? This man said nothing. He was silent. So is death going to be silent when he comes for these lands?

Do I not want to move there; to Nova Scotia Lovey?

I also want to go to Russia for one to two weeks. Oh well, only death knows.

Michelle
September 13, 2018

Wow because my dream world is crazy this morning Lovey.

Weird, thus I wish I was in a place all to myself with no children. Truly hope to move soon.

Weird because I had this weird dream with trucks and cars. This truck; trailer type truck had to stop to go up a bridge; then, had to give it all its power to go up the bridge. I said something about that; what the driver had to do to go up the bridge, but it wasn't anything positive.

There was this young white guy beside me now. We could not go in the direction of the trucks. We were blocked from going in that direction, so we had to take another route on the bridge; to the left of us I believe.

When we took the route, there was light blue water beneath us. We had to go into the water to get to where we were going. He, the young white guy just dropped in the water, and worms, (maggots) was in the water. I can't remember if I ended up in the water, but I remember I was holding on to railing of the bridge, and these worms; maggots was all over me. I did not see them on the railing, it was when they were on me that I saw them. Man did I quickly get them off my body. After that ordeal, I ended up in this prep school with young girls. I so do not know what this dream mean, but Lovey, this three-day trip to my brothers I hope will go great for me. I also hope all is fine with my dad and the doctors.

Lovey, I leave me, my families enemies, my health, your enemies, the food I eat, my wealth, truth, instability, in your good and capable hands. Please let no weapon formed against me prosper in any form or spirit. Protect us always.

Michelle
September 13, 2018

Fulfillment Time. The people of this world is suffering more and more from mental illness; instability, financial woes, spiritual annihilation, and so much more.

Oh Lord Lovey, the lies of humans has and have hurt this earth, and all who live here on earth.

Lovey, is anyone truly looking into the chemicals we put in the food we eat?

Is anyone looking into the genetically modified crap we eat?

Lovey, the people of this earth is going crazy hence, the song **_FULFILLMENT TIME_** by Tony Tuff and Smokie Benz.

Wow, because this song is not just for Jamaicans but for the entire global population. Yes, there is a double standard in society hence, **_PSYCHOLOGICAL CONDITIONING_** by the powers at be.

Now tell me Lovey, when a ordinary citizen kill they are branded as murders, but when a soldier kill (s); they are branded as heroes. Are they both not killing; therefore, is the soldier not a murderer as well? Hence Psychology, and the brainwashing done all around. Thus, the system and systems of men; humans is truly corrupt and unfair. Yes truly disrespectful to Life; good and true life; you Lovey.

Michelle
September 13, 2018

Lovey, before I continue, humans truly do not know about the devil and what the devil does.

These things were not foretold by prophets.

No forget that. Man was going to profit/prophet from the demise of humans. Evil did set his and her system in place, and humans took the bait.

The devil did put strife, greed, hate, all that is evil in the hearts of humans thus; ***the psychological, political, sociological, theological, conditioning that is done globally by the profits; woops the prophets of men.***

Therefore, evil did prophet/profit off humans.

Evil did spread it's wings and seed through the loins of men therefore, women laid with unclean beasts; men and did procreate with these unclean beasts. Thus evil did spread, and many are paying the price today due to the unclean seeds; children of men and women.

All was put into place by the wicked and evil to take humans from life thus, evil did prey on man's; the psyche of humans.

Man did give humans religion. Told them of prophets without knowing that the prophets these evil people that wrote the bible meant was them; evil propheting/profiting off them.

Same word different spelling people, it's just you that could not put it together to educate you on a higher and true scale and or, level.

Michelle
October 15, 2018

And no Lovey, no one better come to me with their justification of soldiers.

YOU CANNOT JUSTIFY MURDER.

You cannot justify going against Life; Lovey and or, God.

You cannot make war and strife with another land then go into that land, and murder the people of that land and vise versa.

No one, absolutely no one can USE TRUTH; GOD; GOOD GOD AND ALLELUJAH, for whom I call Lovey to justify their evil, and nasty ways.

Yes, the White Race is trying hence the nasty beginning given to humans; their bible of whoredom, lies, and deceit Lovey, but death is truly not you Lovey, and never will be. The White Race based on hue, and evil deeds give and sell death, but the Black Race, **TRUE BLACK RACE cannot do this.** They cannot, and must not sell death. They must tell the truth at all times. Good and true life they must have, and continue to have including create all the time.

Lovey, true life is worth it, but the wicked and evil cannot see this therefore, they destroy all in their path and pathway, due to greed, their so-called **DEVELOPMENT.**

Michelle
September 13, 2018

Look pon dem Lovey.
Coo pan dem.

Lovey, do you truly look upon them that run the different lands globally?

Do you even look upon the different corporations of the globe?

No Lovey truly tell me. Earth has truly become the cesspool of sin for humans and spirit yet, humans cannot see this.

We as humans are the ones to build evil.

We as humans are the ones to maintain and sustain evil with our sin, and sins, the products we buy, endorse, people we listen to; say are our role models, emulate, and so much more. So Lovey, if humans do not support good; the good and true; how can we and this earth prosper?

Lovey, how can good prevail if all humans know and or, believe in are lies.

Lovey, why man doa?

Lovey, why man; males had to take truth from all including females?

I know, I did not phrase the question correctly Lovey, why dem; males?

Lovey, why do White People based on hue and evil deeds have to sell their wicked agenda globally?

Dem wicked een!!!!!!!!!!!!!!!

Wow!!!!!!!!!!!!!

Michelle
September 13, 2018

Postscript:

And yes, I know not all Whites based on hue is wicked; so please don't go there.

Michelle

The tears are coming Lovey, because truly woe be unto those that set this man up. Therefore, the **<u>BLACK DEVILS IN THE BLACK COMMUNITY GLOBALLY ARE REAL.</u>**

Many in the Black Community will forever be crocodiles fi real. No wonder a crocodile sits at the head of the Jamaican people. **<u>See the Jamaica coat of arms.</u>**

Evil will forever sit at the head of the Black Man's table Lovey. None in Jamaica cannot see the evils they have done, and accepted.

Therefore, BUJU BANTON had to be set up for death.

Fidem Obeah real fi real.

MY PEN – Buju Banton – Mark Myrie

My Pen, My Pen, this song is real for me Lovey, because parents do not realize that the lies they hand down to their children is passed on by their children to their children. The cycle of lies continue unless we break the chain of lies now.

<u>Lovey, what children can be saved if they are given lies to carry on from generation unto generation?</u> Therefore, for the many; billions; the truth of life must be buried. Humans must not know the truth of life because this is the will of many in this world where lies must take precedence over the truth.

Optimistic Soul – Buju Banton
Close one Yesterday – Buju Banton
Circumstances – Buju Banton

Not An Easy Road – Buju Banton

His load is truly heavy because the devil did take him out whilst sending propaganda, and false recordings around to confuse, and keep this man locked in the jail of Babylon. Dem choa blow, and blow ketch. Thus, all who set this man up is doomed; condemned and rightfully so. Their children and children's children, and future generations must go to hell forevermore without end.

This I know.

The spiritual world has spoken and will see them; all of them that set this man up in hell for real. Trust me, this is more than guaranteed, but the infinite and indefinite truth without end.

Michelle
October 15, 2018

I truly need to end this book.

I have more dreams that I have, but I am going to put these dreams in book six.

My mind is saying continue with this book, but I truly do not want to.

I am going against my spirit.

Book Six I am hoping is not controversial.

People I am lazy and truly do not want to type my notes anymore.

Lazy am I, and lazy I will be for now.

It's bleak outside, and I am truly lazy. I so do not want to go to my father's house, but I have to. He's got a test to do in the morning, and after that I have a doctor's appointment, and another appointment after that. My spirit and mood is so down that I truly do not know what song I can listen to to lift my spirit.

Going to try to type the rest of my dreams and avoid putting these dreams in a book six because they are over a month old.

And yes, I did manage to continue on with this book. I am so lazy and, so not into this book.

Oh well; lazy am I.

Michelle
October 15th, 2018

Aye sa. Life nuh easy at all.

Dreamt Paul.

In the dream he came to my house, hugged me, and was crying. He was sorry for all that happened to us. I think he asked me for forgiveness in the dream. Nonetheless, he got my baby blanket, the one my dog use to use as a blanket. People, my true family and people, wow. Di blanket was not clean, and he had it around him. So I truly do not know what's going on in Paul's life because I did sever the friendship indefinitely.

Am I concerned about Paul?

Truthfully?

No.

Do not lie to me …….. you know what forget it. Let the past stay in the past. What he did never worked, and I so have to truly thank Lovey for securing my son.

Is this dream a dream in a dream?

Yes

My niece need to clean her life and act up. The crap of shit she's doing is wrong. You cannot live above your means; you will fail. Nor, can you pay most of the bills if you have a man living with you. Share the rent and bills come on now. What's the point of having a man in your life if he cannot help you financially. Yes, been there done that hence, freeloaders are carry goh bring dung.

Elevate not descend.

Stress is real, so why kill yourself financially, health wise, sex wise to be in a relationship that is of no true value to you.

Stress is a bitch, so why stay in stress? Get the hell out and stay out.

I see where I want to move to and come September, October, I am going to see these places with my eldest son by the good and true grace of Lovey; God.

Michelle
August 27, 2018

Lovey, this dream this morning with me in Africa. I can't remember the full dream but this African leader, Kenyan leader was speaking. Oh man, I can't remember the part with me and the kids in Africa but nonetheless, the leader of Kenya and or, this man dressed in White; Black Man, tall was speaking. He had kinky hair. I interrupted his speech and told him not all African countries will be saved. Think council Lovey. I was with a council of men and women.

<u>When I said not all of Africa will be saved; the ladies of the council was happy and said yes. They knew not all of Africa was going to be saved.</u> I continued to talk, and some of the men; people left. I guess in the dream they did not want to hear the truth because I was preaching and or, speaking the truth about you Lovey, and telling them you are not with any Muslim, or Islamic land.

I was telling them you cannot say you are of peace and kill; go against life; you Lovey. **_"THOU SHALT NOT KILL, AND HUMANS SHOULD NOT KILL HUMANS."_**

I also told them of respect because none in the Islamic community respect life; you Lovey. So yes, they did not want to hear this, and the fact that no Muslim is saved with the exception of my mother who converted, but who is saved because she is one of my saved. And me after learning the truth begged you for forgiveness when it came to my world of religion, and participating and partaking in religion. Lovey in truth, I cannot let my mother die with them. Therefore, we can no longer be "lambs going to the slaughter house of death." *Islam*

REDEMPTION SONG by Bob Marley

EXODUS by Bob Marley

Yes, you took us out of Islam because this way of life became tainted; dirty due to us letting the devil and their children in. Thus, you found a better way of life for us.

Our original way was no longer peaceful and true to life Lovey. Yes, the truthful ones before the change due to dirty people sabotaging our way of life is saved, **BUT FOR THE NOW ISLAMIC KINGDOM, NONE IS SAVED, AND I KNOW THIS FOR REAL.**

Therefore, I tell you Lovey, impenetrable frameworks and foundations where the devil cannot get in physically, spiritually, universally, beyond the universe, and more we must have between you, and our good and true people more than infinitely and indefinitely more than forever ever without end. We cannot destroy life anymore lovey.

We must also have these impenetrable foundations and frameworks in our physical and spiritual DNA Lovey.

We cannot continue to babysit the wicked and evil. Evil need to go; die now come on now. Let evil go period. Evil is destructive; therefore, we cannot continue to let the wicked and evil of this world dominate and control; ruin all life here on earth.

Look at the way humans; wicked and evil humans have and has destroyed and polluted the waters; waterways and lands of life.

Look how many trees they've destroyed, and have not replaced.

An Lovey; sum a dem plant nasty inorganic trees; meaning, genetically modified crap. So how can you trust man; humans if humans are truly not clean; good?

Getting back to my dream and me preaching; speaking. After all that, the Kenyan leader came to me and I told him. **"IF I AM THE SAVING GRACE FOR HUMANITY; KENYA IS SAVED"** because of what Lucy did for my family. Her family stood surety for me, and my family. We had no place to go and her family stood surety for us. Therefore, Kenya is saved, and that Lovey knows this.

We hugged, and I began to cry. He also showed me the "MAP OF AFRICA." The Map of Africa looked like the pendant of a woman. You know the one Jamaicans wear around their neck and draw Lovey.

He was showing me the lands that were reserved for Americans. Yes, you could see Saudi Arabia on the map, but this land; Saudi Arabia was not included in the lands that was reserved for Americans. The lands were more like Morocco. I want to say East Africa, but I do not have a map of the world before me. When I am editing this book I will look at the map of the world on the computer and tell of the lands if I don't forget. *And at typing what I wrote in word October 15, 2018 I've forgotten the lands.*

I ALSO TOLD THE KENYAN LEADER THAT I WOULD SAVE THE LAND OF JAMAICA, BUT NOT THE PEOPLE BECAUSE THE PEOPLE OF

JAMAICA IS TOO WICKED; VILE. I WANTED TO ASK THE KENYAN LEADER WHY LANDS WERE RESERVED IN AFRICA FOR AMERICANS, BUT WOKE UP OUT OF MY SLEEP.

Lovey, why would this man; Kenyan leader dressed in white reserve and or, show me lands that were reserved for Americans?

<u>Lovey, Mother Africa do not want the people she let go back in her lands; so why would this man; Black Man defy her?</u>

What has Black Americans done to save Africa?

And, don't go there Lovey. Saying you are African American isn't saving Africa, it just makes you ignorant and stupid; truly uneducated and backwards. YOU KNOW NOT THE TRUTH OF LIFE, AND YOUR ORIGINS LOVEY when you say you are African American come on now.

NOT ALL BLACK PEOPLE CAME FROM AFRICA.

Africa is the womb and center of life, nor was Africa the beginning of life because life resided everywhere.

Meaning, BLACK PEOPLE RESIDED EVERYWHERE ON LAND BEFORE THE WHITE PEOPLE CAME INTO BEING.

BLACK PEOPLE CREATED LIFE; meaning, true and good life came from you Lovey thus, TRUE CREATION SEE THE DIFFERENCE BETWEEN CREATION, AND PROCREATION. Therefore, true life cannot die.

Yes, I need to see more when it comes to creation and procreation Lovey. Yes, there is something missing for me because I cannot figure this out.

Why creation and procreation Lovey?

How did evil get so out of hand?

Why wasn't evil contained?

Why have an imbalance when it comes to life here on earth?

I know good and evil came from the Blackness or Darkness; well Blackness of life, but why Lovey?

Was that Blackness good in the first place?
Was that Blackness you?

No, it can't be because truth cannot be evil.
Truth cannot change. So, what am I missing when it comes to this Blackness?

Why am I contradicting myself when it comes to this Blackness?

Is this Blackness not life; good life Lovey?

Let me leave this alone. But Lovey, why would this Kenyan leader reserve and or, show me lands reserved for Americans?

Now tell me Lovey, are you going to permit this because if you are, I will be more than categorically angry, and pissed off at you.

Look at America now.

What has Black Americans done for Mother Africa positively, economically, spiritually, **TRUTHFULLY?**

No, this man cannot reserve anywhere in Africa for Americans because Americans; Black Americans did set up Marcus Mosiah Garvey when he tried to help them with the BACK, OR "BLACK" TO AFRICA MOVEMENT. I say, "Black" to Africa movement Lovey; that sounds better to me. So because Black America rejected Marcus Mosiah Garvey, you Lovey and Mother Africa cannot under ay circumstance (s) reserve a place for Americans. You don't set up your own for failure.

YOU LOVEY WAS TRYING TO PROTECT AMERICANS FROM WHAT IS TO COME. Therefore, I said in some of my earlier books; "LIFE CAME TO LIFE, AND LIFE REJECTED LIFE."

You sent a saviour to America Lovey and Blacks; our own Blacks rejected him by setting him up.

Yes, not all I know.

So why now should he, this man reserve a place in Africa for the ignorant and stupid; *"SELL OUT BLACKS OF AMERICA."*

<u>WHO THE CAP FIT</u> by Bob Marley.

<u>IF BLACK AMERICANS WANT SAVING, LET THEM TRULY EARN IT.</u>

<u>LET THEM TRULY EARN YOUR GRACE AND MERCY LOVEY.</u>

And Lovey, no weapons or weapon formed against me can, or must prosper.

Yes, I know I have family in the country. Family that was born in the land. If they want passage to a better land and life; save them, but I refuse to save Americans on a whole because they are truly not my people.

Ignorance cannot save you. You gave them; "BLACK AMERICANS A WAY OUT, AND THEY REJECTED YOUR OFFERING *Lovey, so why now; why save them?*

<u>Yes, save those who truly want to be saved. I will not be unjust, but you cannot bring ignorance to Africa come on now Lovey.</u>

Africa got rid of the bullshit of crap some of these people's ancestors did.

TRULY DO NOT RETURN EVIL BACK TO AFRICA.
You cannot be vindictive in this way.

Africa did close the door to evil, so let the door stay indefinitely closed to evil.

Mama Africa has enough problems of her own to take on more evil from children of her ancient sell outs, and deceivers.

You Lovey need to find better and true ways to contain all evil because the methods you have in place are truly not working in my book.

Americans are bullies.

LOOK AT THE WAY BLACK AMERICANS FIGHT TO STAY IN A SYSTEM THAT TRULY DON'T LIKE THEM.

Soh mek dem tan Lovey.

If a system don't like you, create good and true systems for your own people.

GET OUT OF THE ABUSE AND HATRED.

STOP WITH THE; MY ANCESTORS BUILT THIS LAND BECAUSE YOUR ANCESTORS DID NOT BUILD ANYTHING.

MEANING, YOUR ANCESTORS KILLED YOUR ASS.

MADE SURE YOUR ASS WAS BORN INTO ABUSE; SLAVERY.

<u>Many of them were raped and robbed therefore, many of your ancestors were born to rapist, abusers, and murderers.</u>

Therefore, I tell you; <u>**"WHEN YOU GIVE UP GOD AND OR, LOVEY, IT'S BY ANY MEANS NECESSARY. GOD AND OR, LOVEY TRULY DO NOT CARE HOW THE DEVIL USE AND ABUSE YOU. YOU ARE NOT LOVEY'S AND OR, GOD'S CONCERN."**</u>

Meaning, you and or, your ancestors walked away from life; so life has closed the door to you. Therefore, the devil and or, the wicked and evil can do whatever they want with you; including <u>**KILL YOU.**</u>

YOU GAVE UP LIFE THEREFORE, YOU ARE NOT APART OF LIFE ANYMORE.

So, truly don't complain how the devil and their children beat you, use and abuse you. You made the choice; your ancestors made the choice to walk away from good and true life; now pay the price, and keep paying the price for your disobedience, and your ancestors disobedience.

- ✓ *You cannot give up life and want it back. There are no givesy backsy in life. Once you give up life it's gone because your name is taken out of the BOOK OF LIFE AND PUT IN THE BOOK OF DEATH.*

Therefore, from generation unto generation your name is in the book of death. Meaning, no children of death can be redeemed. Some of you can thank your ancestors for this.

Many of your ancestors were born to thieves and murderers.

THINK!!!!!!!!!!!!!!!!!

Why were so many Blacks taken; sold into slavery?

Do you even know what slavery is?
Do you even know what constitutes slavery?

Your wicked and evil ancestors had to be evicted from Africa. You were to break; contaminate the other Blacks of the world.

Know the truth. You can save your ancestors form hell, but many of you are so backwards and ignorant that many of you truly cannot be saved, or have a saving grace.

"WAKE UP"

TRUTH IS by Duane Stephenson

Michelle
September 09, 2018 and October 2018

Wow Lovey, what's going on in the Cayman Islands with he government?

This dream this morning August 28, 2018 wow.

Dreamt I was in the Cayman Islands. My sister bought me a ticket, but with her buying my ticket; I did not know where I was going to stay.

In the dream Donna lent me her cell phone. I do not know if it was a Samsung or, iPhone, but it was big. Not as big as my Tab E, but nonetheless big, and it was in a black and silver case.

Oh man, I do not want to get into this dream because it's long and it entails family Lovey. All in all; after leaving the beach where I was, I hooked up with my cousin, and we went back to her place where she was picking mangoes for this black lady, and I began to pick mangoes for her too. I picked the first mango for the black lady that did not like me I thought. She did not have a pleased look on her face.

Oh man, I need to tell the entire dream from beginning. The black farmer man that liked me. Her; my cousin's son was also in the mango tree picking mangoes. He was in the tree, and I went under the tree to pick mangoes. I was a bit scared because I did not want any of the mangoes to hit me in my head. At any rate picking mangoes and picking enough mangoes, one of the ripe mangoes I had fell in someone's back yard. Then I saw this other mango tree. It had ripe mangoes on it as well as bloom. Someone had picked a mango off the tree, but it had dropped on the ground. One the mango; bitten mango where the flesh; small piece of flesh was seen, I believe there was a fly. I was so happy the tree was blooming, and had ripe mangoes. I wanted to hug the tree and bless it. I did not get to hug the tree, or pick any mangoes off the tree, but I was praying for the mango tree. I also wanted to cry.

See the mango tree I had told in real life that when I came back to the Cayman Islands she had better have mangoes on her to eat, and in the dream the mango tree provided fruits; small ripe mangoes, and was blooming. So because the mango tree listened, I blessed her. But in blessing her, the weird part of this was. It was as if I should not bless the mango tree. Something did not want me to bless the tree so they; I truly don't know who tied up di mango tree. You know how you would put a bag around a tree and tie it up for the winter. Well it's the same way with this tree; mango tree, and the tree became small. My cousin was also beside the mango tree that was now small and tied up.

After that happened, this young white boy looked at her funny. Trust me, I don't know where the boy came from or, where the complex they were in came from. My cousin got offended by the look of this young boy and said; excuse me, we are black, and you are on a black island. *(Do not quote me on the exact words, but it was like that.)*

She was angry, and we walked towards the boy and silver coins around the size of a Canadian dime fell on the ground. I cannot tell you how many coins fell from my cousin. Nor can I tell you if the coins fell from her pocket.

Trust me an argument ensued, and the boys mother intervened and tried to squash things, but it only got worse. Oh man, I can't remember if the young boy used the word Niggers.

At any rate, males; older males; white men got into the action of being racist to the point where I called one a wanker. I wanted to call the older ugly looking white man a raw pig, but ended up calling him a wanker instead.

Somehow the white boy's mother knew I called them a wanker because she said something to the effect of her knowing I used the word wanker.

I can't remember if my cousin said she was going to talk to her government official about this, or if I suggested for her to do so. But this family did not care. We left. We; my cousin and I did not get far but officials; the Prime Minister was laying in wait for us. Oh man, I believe there was a champagne bottle on the ground beside his jeep. See the Prime Minister knew what happened before we could even call him. Thus, he was waiting and or, lying in wait for us in his jeep to hurt me and my cousin.

They tried to hurt us, and I said; don't worry im a goh dead. Don't quote me on the don't worry, but quote me on **_he's going to die._** Meaning, the Prime Minister is going to die because he took a bribe from these white people to hurt his black own. When I said; he's going to die; the jeep he was in flipped over with them; the Prime Minister in it.

Now there was a jeep that was with us and the young man and or, my cousin did not want to take the road before us.

So yes, this is a dream in a dream.

Is someone in the government of the Cayman Islands taking bribes from wealthy white people?

IT WOULD SEEM SO, AND THEY WOULD HURT YOU TO PROTECT THEIR BACK-DOOR DEALINGS. THUS, IT NEVER FAILS AS TO HOW GOVERNMENTS; BLACK SO-CALLED GOVERNMENTS WOULD SELL OUT THEIR LAND/COUNTRY AND PEOPLE FOR MONEY.

Bunch of f-ing scums that respect not their land and people.

<u>Bunch of f-ing sell outs. No wonder Black Lands cannot be better due to the sell outs; BLACK SELL OUTS GLOBALLY.</u>

Listen Lovey, you know I have absolutely no respect for Black Political Leaders, and People that sell off Black Lands to foreign investors that rape the land and people of their value and self worth.

Now you said you wanted a home in the Cayman Islands, and look at what's happening in the government there. <u>**So, if this being the case; the government of the Cayman Islands taking bribes, and tainting the land; then find someplace else to set up shop; go.**</u>

<u>**Do not make the Cayman Islands your home anymore. Take your blessing more than infinitely and indefinitely from the island. Black Lands need to become clean, and stay clean come on now.**</u>

<u>**I AM SO FRIGGING FED UP OF THESE DISGUSTING BLACK POLITICIANS THAT SELL**</u>

OUT AND SELL OFF THE LAND ONLY TO ALLOW RACIST SCUMBAGS, AND DOUCHE BAGS TO COME IN AND BELITTLE THE PEOPLE; AS WELL AS RAPE THE LAND AND PEOPLE OF THEIR SELF WORTH, AND SELF RESPECT. ENOUGH IS ENOUGH COME ON NOW.

Lovey, **_CRAZY BALDHEAD_** by Bob Marley.

Come on Lovey, let's chase those Crazy Baldhead's out of town. Lovey, you and I know that you would never give your power to a Bald Head, so let's renew the True Black Race and live; truly live from here on in.

Michelle

It's 5:32 am Lovey and I don't want to leave my bed; home. It's cold outside; well I don't know how cold it is outside, but the cold my body cannot take period. I dread going outside because my feet keep acting up and I have to take my dad to the doctors today, and Thursday with today being September 11, 2018.

My nephew is working so he can't take us, and I asked my second child, but he said he really doesn't want to because he does not know my dad, and he (my dad) never did anything for him. Which is true. My dad has never done anything for any of my children, nor does my dad know them. My dad was never around them, nor has my dad ever said happy birthday to them. So yes, I can over stand why he does not want to help my dad. Like he said, if it was me it would be different.

I need to go see my different doctors but can't. Helping my dad to sort himself out. But, I so do not want to go out their in the cold.

Lovey, why am I dreaming about Americans?

Just dreamt Buffalo had a basket ball team, and the team was plagued with injuries. They had so much players on their roster, and many of them were injured to the point where the team became a joke. I believe I asked in the dream why there's so many players on the team and LeBron James was explaining to me why.

So I do not know if a lot more players in basketball is going to get injured. I know Buffalo has a hockey and football team, but not a basketball team. There is the Boston Celtics in basketball. But I will not worry about this because I truly do not like basketball in that way. And yes, in the dream I wanted to tell LeBron I did not like the sport.

Is there more to this dream?

Yes

The procession of players and this white girl walking in the procession with the players.

Am I missing something else?

Yes

So, I truly do not know, and I will not speculate on this dream, so I am going to leave things alone because death is real for real.

Michelle
September 11, 2018

September 10th yesterday was weird for me. I dreamt DMX and Eve the rapper. Man, Lovey, DMX need to clean his life up, and sort out his affairs.

In the dream he had ten kids and saying he liked to live a certain lifestyle. He was with someone and was moving his genital area on the woman. He was clothed, and in a dark blue to black pants with this huge mansion; white mansion not too far from them. And no Lovey, I did not see the woman. Thus I woke up saying; **_DMX need to get his life in order._** The odd part of the dream for me was; after seeing what I saw with DMX, and the unseen lady, I saw a yonder version of DMX and Eve the rapper. They were on stage together singing and or, rapping, and Eve dropped the Mic. And all you see was DMX taking the mic and hit Eve. I don't know if something was wrong with Eve and that's why she dropped the mic, but something was odd. Does not sit right, and with me writing these lines on paper something does not sit right with them and this dream. I don't want to speculate, but maybe there are issues with Eve and DMX that go way back. But in the dream it seemed as if it was someone else other than DMX that hit her.

How do I put it?

In the dream it seemed as if it was someone playing DMX. But it's a weird one. Hence I truly do not know which male rapper and or, musical artist in the past that Eve had a run in with, or if she was physically abused by someone; a male artist in the past and is not saying anything.

I so do not know if this is a dream in a dream. So I am definitely going to leave this dream alone because I truly do not know.

Maybe Eve and DMX and or, some male artist is going to tour, and a physical altercation happens. Just speculating even though I don't want to; so let me leave things alone.

Michelle
September 11, 2018

Did I dream Vin Diesel yesterday, with yesterday being September 10th, 2018?

Yes

This Babylonian looking young woman with black hair was clinging to him like a baby would cling to their parent. They had four boys with the last boy looking like Vin Diesel.

The children were young. But the odd part of the dream was; Vin had other children. I think two girls and they were tall with brown skin, and I believe light brown to gold curly hair. Oh man, do not quote me on two tall girls because I can only remember one distinctly. They; the girls were meeting their siblings for the first time.

Am I forgetting something?

Yes

The names of the boys Vin had with the Babylonian looking woman. So I truly do not know if Vin is going to split from his now wife, or girlfriend due to infidelity. Or, maybe he's going to do a movie with kids.

Do not know, and truly do not care because <u>death has a hold of someone; female death that is.</u>

Michelle
September 11, 2018

Wow Lovey.

The weather has changed, and my body has changed. That energy that I would feel early in the morning has left.

Our vibe and vibration has changed too Lovey, but I am not going to worry about that. All I can do is talk to you my way.

And yes, I refuse to worry about Americans.

Oh man, I have to call Margaret, and send DeLavallade, Michael DeLavallade a email.

Hopefully he's okay because he said something to me in the basketball dream. I did not see him; only heard his voice.

Michelle

COMING SOON

MY TALK; CONVERSATION WITH GOD – BOOK THREE

MY WORLD OF DREAMS – BOOK SIX

SEX TALK, AND MORE

BOOKS BY MICHELLE JEAN 2018

MY WORLD OF DREAMS 2018 – BOOK ONE

MY WORLD OF DREAMS 2018 – BOOK TWO

LIFE IS NOT A GAME

IT'S TIME

MY WORLD OF DREAMS 2018 – BOOK THREE

MY TALK LA – MY LOS ANGELES VACATION 2017

MY WORLD OF DREAMS 2018 – BOOK FOUR

MY TALK; COVERSATION WITH GOD – BOOK ONE

MY TALK; CONVERSATION WITH GOD – BOOK TWO